M is for Monkey

Kelly Kauffman

© 2014 by TGS International, a wholly owned subsidiary of Christian Aid Ministries, Berlin, Ohio.

All rights reserved. No part of this book may be used, reproduced, or stored in any retrieval system, in any form or by any means, electronic or mechanical, without written permission from the publisher except for brief quotations embodied in critical articles and reviews.

ISBN: 978-1-941213-47-6

Cover and layout design: Violet Hershberger

Printed in the USA

Published by:
TGS International
P.O. Box 355
Berlin, Ohio 44610 USA
Phone: 330-893-4828
Fax: 330-893-2305
www.tgsinternational.com

TGS000911

M is for Monkey

Once upon a time my family and I lived in Liberia. Liberia is a poor country in West Africa and looks very different from America. It's a warm country with lots of rain and forests.

In America, many people like to have pets. What kind of pets do you have? A dog? A cat? Maybe you even have a pet lizard!

People in Liberia like to have pets too. But most of the time they do not have a dog or a cat. They have another kind of pet animal. Can you guess what it is?

If you guessed a monkey, you are right!

One day Micah, one of our missionary friends, called and asked, "Would you like to have a monkey?"

What would you have said?

You probably would have said, "Yes!"

That's just what we said.

Several years before moving to Liberia, we went to a zoo in America. We stood at the monkey pen for a long time and watched the monkeys holler

and jump around. Now, in Liberia, we were going to have our very own monkey. We were so excited! We could hardly wait for Micah to bring us the monkey.

Finally one day Micah brought Tinker to our house. We ran

outside to see her. She was still a baby m o n k e y, so she was tiny. She was brown and had big eyes— big brown eyes that blinked curiously at us.

Did you know that a monkey's hand looks like your own hand? That's right!

They have hands with five fingers, and they even have fingernails just like you. Their feet look like our hands too. God created them in this special way to help them climb trees and peel and eat fruit.

He knew exactly how to create their bodies.

We found out that Tinker loved to be held. She loved to snuggle up to us, just like a baby likes to cuddle up to her mom. When we sat down to read a book, she would jump onto our laps. She even went on bike rides with us!

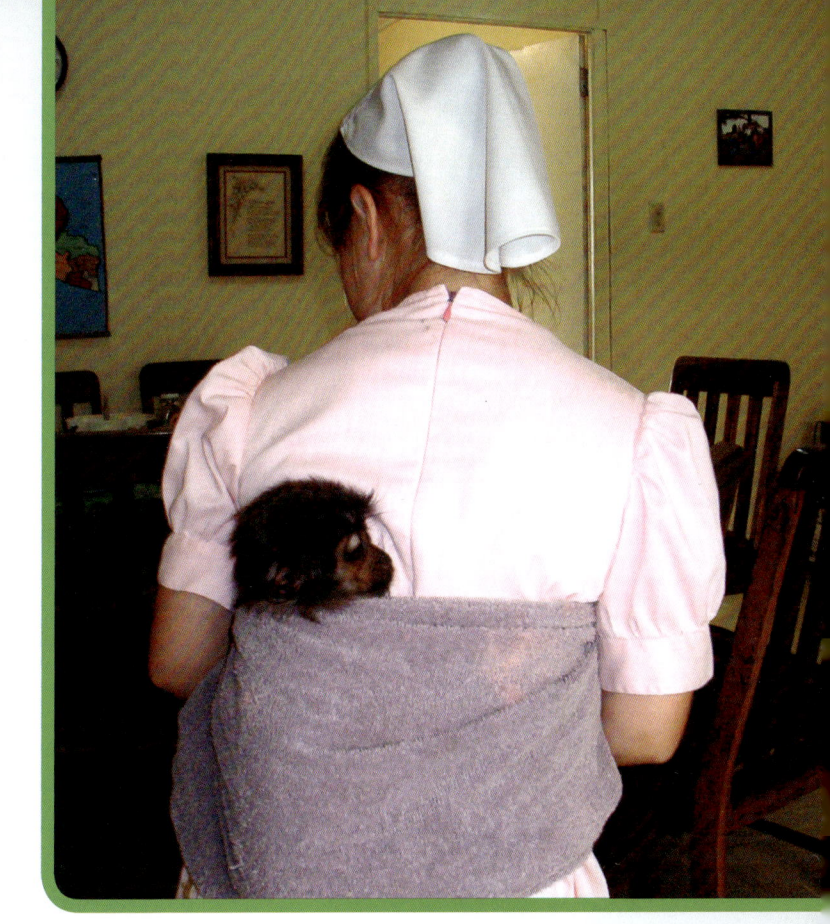

In Liberia the people don't push their babies around in strollers. They tie their babies onto their backs with a piece of fabric to keep the baby secure.

One day my sister wanted to see if Tinker would like to ride on her back. She tied Tinker onto her back with a piece of fabric and walked around like that for a while. Tinker liked it so much that she went to sleep.

Tinker loved to cuddle the baby kittens we had at our place. Sometimes that was okay, but other times it put the kittens in danger. You see, Tinker was tied with a rope to a pole in our garage. By climbing up the pole, she could go all the way up to the roof. Tinker liked to sleep all the way at the top.

One day we looked out the window and saw Tinker holding a kitten on the roof. We laughed because it looked so funny! But we were scared that Tinker would drop the kitten, so we scrambled up and brought the kitten back down.

Some little children like to hold onto a blanket to go to sleep. Tinker was getting to be a big monkey, but she still liked to hold onto something when she went to sleep. Of course, she liked to hold the kittens.

But sometimes the kittens would not be around for Tinker to hold. Can you guess what she held onto then? She found an old soccer ball and cuddled up to that! Do you think a small monkey can hold a big ball? No, of course not! Tinker found out that a ball that rolls away is not a good blankie. One day she found something that was better than a ball or a kitten. Can you guess what that was?

It was a baby monkey!

Someone came to our place and asked if we wanted

another monkey. We did want another monkey so that Tinker wouldn't be so lonely. We called this little monkey Sassy. For a long time Sassy was very scared. I will tell you why.

When Sassy had just been born, her mama was killed. Some people who came into the jungle found little Sassy and brought her back with them. Do you know how scared you feel when you have a bad dream? That is how Sassy felt after her mama was killed. She wanted us to hold her all the time. When we tried to put her down, she screamed and jerked around. Do you think that is how a monkey cries?

Tinker was happy that she had another monkey

to hold. She was a very good mama to Sassy, and Sassy was not scared anymore.

When Tinker was the only monkey we had, she stayed tied to her rope. Now that we had another monkey, we had to do something else. My brother built a cage for them

to stay in. Now they could both run loose.

They had a lot of fun in the cage. They jumped all over it. They jumped from the tree to the door. They hung upside down from the top of the cage. Sometimes we thought it would be fun to be a monkey.

Most of the time it was fun to have two monkeys

instead of only one. But we found out that if you put two monkeys together, they help each other get into mischief. Did you ever hear someone say, "double trouble"? Well, Tinker and Sassy were exactly that. They liked to help each other find or make holes to escape from the cage. Since Sassy was so much smaller than Tinker, she would usually slip out through the holes. Sometimes a hole was big enough for Tinker to come out too.

When they would get out of the pen, they would be very, very naughty. They would tear up books. They would find keys and run away

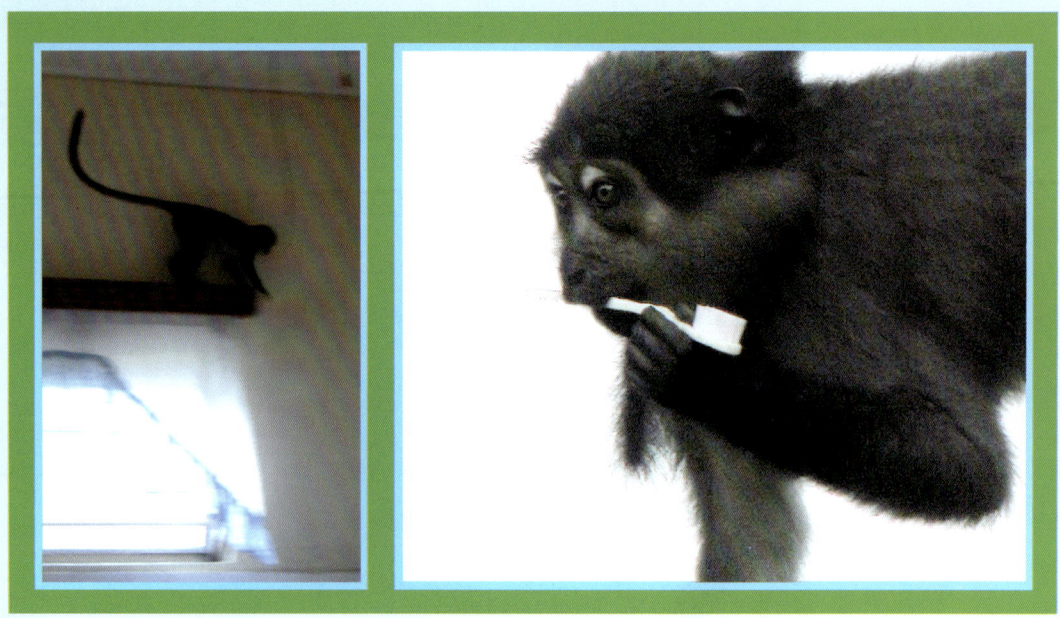

with them. Tinker even went into the bathroom and found a toothbrush one time! Sometimes they would go down to the neighbors and steal their rice. One time Sassy opened the door to our house and ran around in the kitchen.

By now you may be wondering, What do monkeys eat? Monkeys eat lots and lots of fruit. They love bananas, pineapples, oranges, and any kind of fruit they can find. But they also love treats that people make.

When Tinker and Sassy would break out of their cage, we would try to get them back in by throwing their favorite foods into their cage. They liked cake, and they liked bread with jam on it. They liked to eat the jam off the bread and the frosting off the cake—just like some little children I know. Sometimes they even got to eat treats that came from America.

Sometimes Tinker and Sassy got mad. They made hissing and spitting noises and showed their teeth. The skin right above Tinker's eyes would get white and her ears would wiggle back and forth.

When you get dirty, how do you clean yourself? You take a bath or a shower, right?

But monkeys are animals, not people. Do you know how they stay clean? They pick through each other's hair, looking for bugs and fleas. If they find some, they

will eat them because they like bugs. They even looked through the dog's hair for fleas! When we played with them, they looked over our arms for bugs. Thankfully, they never found any.

Tinker and Sassy loved to tease our dogs. They liked to

jump all over them. The dogs would tease the monkeys too. They all had fun playing together.

One day we had to say goodbye to Tinker and Sassy. We were going to move back to America, and we could not take them along. We were very sad, but we were glad some nice people took them to their homes.

Maybe someday you will be able to have your own pet monkey. Wouldn't that be fun?

The End

The Kauffman siblings. Kelly is on the left.

About the Author

At the age of fourteen, Kelly Kauffman moved to Liberia with her parents and three siblings. She has never regretted spending four of her teen years there. Kelly currently lives in Thomaston, Georgia, where she and her family are involved in a church-planting endeavor. She works at her family's deli and loves to interact with the customers. When not working, she enjoys reading, traveling, and spending time with friends, both big and little.